HANDMADE
Christmas
ORNAMENTS

Designer and Contributing Writer

Jane Johnston

Publications International, Ltd.

Jane Johnston is a crafts designer who obtained her Bachelor of Arts degree in Studio Arts from the University of Pittsburgh. She has supplied many hand-made Christmas ornaments to retail stores throughout southwestern Pennsylvania. Ms. Johnston is also a member of the Craftsman's Guild of Pittsburgh.

PHOTOGRAPHY:
Sacco Productions Limited/Chicago

PHOTOGRAPHERS:
Ken Hyne, Tom O'Connell, Peter Ross

PHOTO STYLISTS:
Linda Banach, Paula Walters

PHOTO PRODUCTION:
Roberta Ellis
Models/Royal Model Management:
Theresa Lesniak, Monica Magdziak

The brand-name products mentioned in this publication are service marks or trademarks of their respective companies. The mention of products in directions is merely a record of the procedure used and does not constitute an endorsement by the respective proprietors of Publications International, Ltd., nor does it constitute an endorsement by any of these companies that their products should be used in the manner recommended by this publication.

ISBN: 1-4127-1068-5

Contents

Introduction
Steps to Success 4

Crafting handmade Christmas ornaments can be great family fun or an exciting activity for friends of all ages to enjoy. Making your own ornaments can help put the warmth and heart back into a season that, for some, has become "too much." The gift of a handmade ornament says you care enough to spend time on someone special. Give a child an ornament that you have made, and he or she will remember you every time the ornament is hung on a Christmas tree in years to come. For a little something special to give to your friends and neighbors, a handmade ornament is just the right gift.

Some Basic Tools

Glue. In most cases, craft glue and hot glue guns can be used interchangeably, but there are differences. Craft glue takes longer to set up, or establish a bond. Hot glue is better if you don't want to hold something in place for a long time or if you don't want to wait between steps while the glue dries. However, craft glue bonds better than hot glue on surfaces that are nonporous (such as a button surface); craft glue also bonds better when gluing dissimilar surfaces (nonporous buttons to a porous grapevine).

Since hot glue comes out of the gun in a glob, some glue might ooze around the edges of a glued object. In this instance, use a sharp knife or a single-edge razor blade to trim off the excess. By contrast, craft glue is transparent when dry.

When you buy a hot glue gun, consider getting a trigger-action gun, which delivers the smallest amount of glue possible and offers the best control of the nozzle. When using a hot glue gun, let the glue completely cool before getting rid of the annoying "strings" that often appear between the object and the hot glue gun. Finally, let the glue cool completely before releasing the glued object; otherwise, the object may shift position.

When you buy glue, choose one that dries clear and is specifically made for crafts. The glue should be flexible, which is an important feature when you are gluing fabric.

Scissors. Scissors are necessary for preparing almost every project. Be sure your scissors are sharp; otherwise, cutting felt and polyester batting will be difficult. Have one pair of scissors for cutting only fabrics. Cutting hair or paper can quickly dull the blades.

Orange sticks and toothpicks. An orange stick (from your manicure kit) is useful for setting rhinestones. With rhinestones or any of the variety of studs available, the main action is pushing the points on the settings through the material and then bending the points over. Although an orange stick takes a bit longer than a setting machine, it will save you money. Toothpicks are useful for almost every project. Toothpicks can be used to spread glue, to hold things in place, or to push small objects around.

Tweezers. Tweezers are another handy item to keep with your craft tools. They can be used to pick up small objects, such as wiggle eyes.

Batting. For felt ornaments, use batting instead of stuffing. Stuffing often develops clumps, especially when it is being pushed into something. Stuffing also never seems to get into the far corners of the ornament.

Paper twist. Paper twist comes in a variety of widths, depending on the manufacturer. Adjust the directions of a project to reflect different widths. Do not cut the paper twist to the size specified in the directions until you have unraveled and spread it as flat as possible.

Handy Techniques

Glue. Whenever you are gluing something, it is better to put the glue on the object to be placed (if possible) rather than on the surface where the object will end up. This provides better control and prevents the glue from being smeared.

After cutting the stem from a ribbon rose, apply a dab of hot glue to the rear of the flower. The glue will hold the rose together.

If you are gluing a stem, first trim the stem to ¼ inch. Apply glue to the stem by sticking it down the nozzle of the glue gun.

To make leaves appear more lifelike, apply glue to the bottom rear of the leaves only.

To make it look as if there are more flowers, fruit, gift packages, or bears than actually used, glue the first round of items just peeking above the edge of the object. Glue the second row to the first row at a slightly higher level. Glue the third row to the second even higher. Make sure there are no holes where someone can see down into the mound you've created.

Ribbon. When choosing a wide ribbon for a bigger project (such as tree garland), use ribbon with wire in the edges. The wire will help give the ribbon a more graceful line.

Beads. Strings of beads usually come with about 6 inches of extra string on either end. To cut a string of beads, make a knot at one end of the string that is large enough so the beads cannot slip off. Move as many inches of beads as you need down against this knot. Tie another knot just past the last bead and cut the string. Place a dab of craft glue on each knot to prevent unraveling. (To knot a string in a specific spot, first make a loose knot around a straight pin. Then move the pin to the spot where you want the knot. Tighten the string.)

Some General Directions

Several directions apply to different projects: making loopy bows, cutting out patterns, or tying knots.

To make a loopy bow:

1 Cut the ribbon to the specified length.

2 Find an object that is approximately the same diameter as the loop of the bow. (Your fingers can work well for this: one for a small loop, two for a larger loop.)

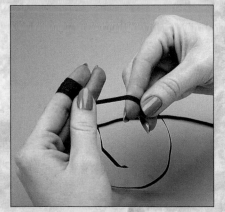

3 Leaving about 1 inch free, wrap the ribbon around the object. Leave another inch free at the end. Cross the two free ends over the loop.

4 Insert a smaller piece of ribbon through all the loops. Bring this ribbon around, and tie it in a knot. Pull the bow from the object, and separate the loops in an attractive arrangement.

To cut out patterns:

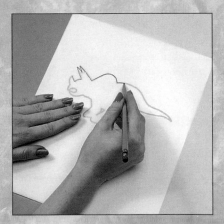

1 Place tracing paper over the pattern. Using a pen or pencil, trace the pattern onto the paper. (Note: You can also photocopy the pattern from the book.)

2 Using rubber cement, bond the tracing paper to a piece of thin cardboard.

3 Cut out the shape, following the traced lines.

To tie an overhand knot:

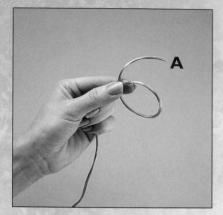

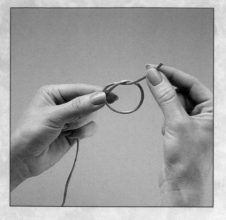

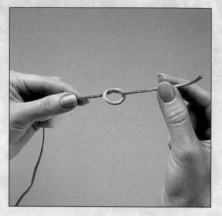

1 Create a loop with your line. Note point A.

2 Pass point A around and through the loop from behind.

3 Pull the line tight.

To tie a square knot:

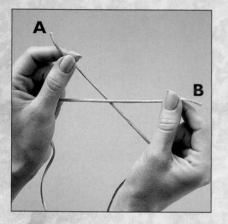

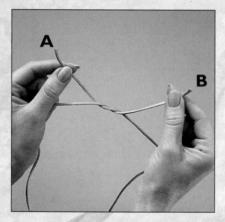

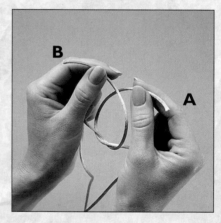

1 Take the two ends of your cord, one in each hand. Place line B in front of line A.

2 Wrap B around A, bringing it behind, then underneath and out the front.

3 Pass B in front of A, forming a loop.

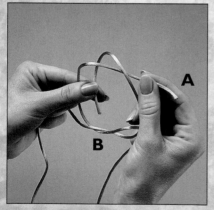

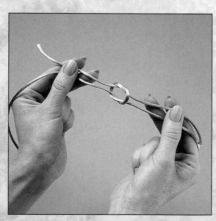

4 Bring B under A, then through the loop and out.

5 Pull the line tight with both hands.

Theme Tree Ideas

Once you've created ornaments for a theme tree, you'll need to think about tree skirts, garlands, and tree toppers to finish decorating your tree.

Victorian Theme Tree. For a tree skirt, use an old set of lacy curtains. For garlands, try 3-inch-wide lace gathered with a bow every 2 to 3 feet. Another option is 3-inch-wide wire-edged ribbon in a pale color. A ball of dried or silk flowers with ribbon trailers works well as a tree topper.

Western Theme Tree. A tree skirt can be made from red and blue bandannas stitched together, or use 3 yards of burlap or cowboy theme fabric. For a garland, use several strands of jute twine gathered in a bow every few feet. Small American flags stuck into the sides of the bows look nice. An alternative garland can be made from bandannas tied together into a string. Make a large star from lightweight aluminum or stitched burlap to serve as a tree topper.

Children's Theme Tree. Instead of a tree skirt, try piling small stuffed animals around the base of the tree. A length of brightly colored flannel would also make a fun tree skirt. Use candy for the garland: a string of cellophane-wrapped gum balls or thick red yarn with candy canes tied in every few feet. A tree topper could be created with a loopy bow made from thick red yarn.

Country Theme Tree. For a tree skirt, start with a 3-yard piece of muslin or brown butcher's paper. Next, cut potato stamps in basic shapes and then stamp the fabric using acrylic paint. A strand of jute twine works well as a garland. Gather the twine in a bow every few feet; stick bright red berries or a holly pick in each side of the bow. Wide gingham wire-edge ribbon gathered in a big loopy bow would make a great tree topper.

How Difficult Is Each Ornament?

The ornament projects vary in difficulty. Many are easy; many are intermediate; and some are difficult. Most of the projects have been designed to be as simple as possible. The easy projects are best suited for beginners. The intermediate and difficult projects use many of the same skills called for in the easy projects, but there are more steps and more parts to put together.

Victorian Theme Tree

Beaded Wreath: easy
Cornucopia of Roses: easy
Hats Off to the Holidays: easy
Royal Yule Ornament: intermediate
Snow Bird: intermediate
Victorian Angel: difficult

Western Theme Tree

Festive Bolo: easy
Holly Badge: easy
Pepper Yule Party: easy
Red-Hot Wreath: easy
Christmas Kerchief: intermediate
Cowgirl Hat: intermediate
On the Christmas Trail: intermediate
Texas Santa: intermediate

Children's Theme Tree

Bears on a Sleigh Ride: easy
Christmas Olé: easy
Pom-Pom Snowman: easy
Dinosaur in December: intermediate
Noel Rocking Horse: intermediate

Country Theme Tree

Buttons 'n' Eyelet Wreath: easy
Old-Fashioned Butter Mold: easy
Country Christmas Goose: intermediate
Holiday Holstein: intermediate
Jute Twist: intermediate
Old World St. Nick: difficult

Individual Ornaments

And a Partridge in a . . . : easy
Braided Candy Cane: easy
Dove of Peace: easy
Joy to the World: easy
Santa's Sleigh: easy
Angel of the Vine: intermediate
Cross-Stitch Christmas: intermediate
O Christmas Tree!: intermediate
Bountiful Santa: difficult
Button-Down Santa: difficult
Jolly Clay Santa: difficult
Yuletide Bauble: difficult

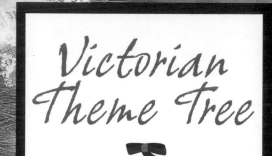

Victorian Theme Tree

Imagine yourself in an earlier time, and catch the feeling of Christmas past with a Victorian theme tree. Cornucopias, lace, and pastels will bring the look and feel of this refined era to all your Christmas celebrations. Turn to the Introduction for ideas on Victorian garlands, skirts, and tree toppers.

Royal Yule Ornament

What You'll Need

12×12-inch blue fabric • Scissors • 3-inch-diameter foam ball • Sequin pins • 40¼ inches antique gold trim • 32 inches blue satin ribbon, ⅛ inch wide • 32 inches gold satin ribbon, ⅛ inch wide • Tape measure or yardstick • Hot glue gun, glue sticks • 5-inch gold tinsel tassel

1 Copy and cut out pattern on page 64. (See page 5 for directions on cutting out patterns.) On fabric bias, cut 7 pattern pieces from blue fabric.

2 Attach 7 pieces of fabric to foam ball with pins. Pieces should be evenly distributed around ball and edges will overlap slightly.

3 Measure and cut gold trim into seven 4¾-inch lengths and two 3½-inch lengths. Cut blue ribbon into a 24-inch length and an 8-inch length. Cut gold ribbon into same lengths as blue ribbon.

4 Cover overlapping fabric edges with 4¾-inch lengths of gold trim; secure with pins. Hot glue trim in place, removing pins as you glue.

5 Glue a 3½-inch length of gold trim in a circle to top of ball and other to bottom, covering trim ends.

6 Glue tassel to center bottom of gold trim.

7 Overlap 24-inch lengths of blue and gold ribbon. Make a 1-inch-diameter loopy bow. Tie off bow with 8-inch length of blue gold ribbon. (See page 5 for instructions on making a loopy bow.) Glue bow to center of gold trim.

8 To make a hanger, fold 8-inch gold ribbon in half. Glue ends to top of ornament, in middle of loopy bow.

Cornucopia of Roses

What You'll Need

2 yards 3 inches mauve satin ribbon, $1/16$ inch wide • Tape measure or yardstick • Scissors • 5-inch crocheted cone • Hot glue gun, glue sticks • 1 bunch silk dark mauve, brushed gold rosebuds, $3/4$ inch buds • 1 bunch silk light mauve, brushed gold rosebuds, $3/4$ inch buds • Wire cutters • 9 silk rose leaves, $1/2$ inch each

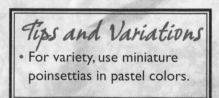

1 Cut ribbon into the following lengths: 9 inch, 12 inch, and three 18 inch.

2 Starting at lowest point of cone mouth, weave 9-inch length of ribbon around top edge. Trim excess ribbon, and spot glue ends in place.

3 Mix dark and light rosebuds. Twist stem ends together and, about 2 inches from bottom of flowers, bend the stems back on themselves so length is less than 3 inches. If necessary, clip stems with wire cutters to shorten.

4 Insert flowers into cone. Spot glue a few roses around cone to hold. Clip stems from rose leaves. Glue leaves into bouquet around edges.

5 To make a hanger, fold the 12-inch length of ribbon in half. Make an overhand knot near open ends. Glue folded end to cone where you started ribbon weaving.

6 Overlap 18-inch ribbon lengths, and make a 2-inch bow. Glue bow on top of hanger end.

Tips and Variations
• For variety, use miniature poinsettias in pastel colors.

Hats Off to the Holidays

What You'll Need

22 clear beads, 8mm each • 4-inch crochet hat • Hot glue gun, glue sticks • 3 glass ball picks, 15mm each • Wire cutters • 2 rose leaves, ½ inch each • 30 inches satin mauve ribbon, ⅛ inch wide • Tape measure or yardstick • 20 inches satin mauve ribbon, ¹⁄₁₆ inch wide

1 Glue 8mm beads around base of hat crown.

2 Clip wires off glass ball picks. Glue glass balls together at crown base, next to 8mm beads.

3 Clip stems from leaves. Glue leaves in an attractive arrangement next to glass balls.

4 Cut ⅛-inch ribbon into two 15-inch lengths. Make a ¾-inch-diameter loopy bow from a 15-inch length of ribbon. Tie off loopy bow with second 15-inch length of ribbon. Trim all ends even. (See page 5 for instructions on making a loopy bow.) Glue bow to side of glass balls.

5 For a hanger, double 20-inch length of ribbon and thread it through brim, a few inches from glass balls. Tie an overhand knot near ends.

Tips and Variations
• Ribbon roses could be used in place of the beads, with larger roses in place of the glass balls.

Snow Bird

What You'll Need

3½-inch wicker birdcage • Paring knife • 5-inch string blue beads, 3mm • Tweezers • Hot glue gun, glue sticks • 2-inch dove • Wire cutters • 18 inches white lace, ½ inch wide • 48½ inches blue ribbon, ⅛ inch wide • Tape measure or yardstick • Scissors • Craft glue

1 Remove tape from bottom of cage. Slip knife between cage bottom and edge. Pop out bottom.

2 Pick up 1 end of bead string with tweezers. Apply hot glue to last bead on string. Reach inside cage, and press glued bead to top of cage until glue sets. Repeat with other end of bead string.

3 Clip wires that stick out from bottom of bird. Prop cage partially upright, and hot glue bird to middle of bead string. (Use tweezers to hold bead string still.) Replace cage bottom.

4 Cut lace into the following lengths: 5½ inch, 4 inch, and 8½ inch. Cut blue ribbon into the following lengths: 4 inch, 8½ inch, and two 18 inch.

8 Glue 8½-inch length of lace to horizontal piece of wood below lace. Trim lace to overlap ¼ inch.

9 Glue 8½-inch of blue ribbon over top of lace placed in step 8. Trim lace to overlap ¼ inch.

6 Glue 4-inch length of lace to edge of solid piece of wood above lace placed in step 5. Trim lace to overlap ¼ inch.

10 Make a double bow with 18-inch lengths of blue ribbon. Hot glue ribbon to cage top, right below hook. Let glue dry completely before hanging.

5 Use craft glue to place all lace and ribbon. Glue 5½-inch length of lace on the wicker bars of the cage, just below solid piece of wood at cage's top. Trim lace to overlap ¼ inch.

7 Glue 4-inch length of blue ribbon over top of lace placed in step 6.

Tips and Variations
• Fill the cage with a bouquet of silk rosebuds instead of a bird for a special rose-lover!

Victorian Angel

What You'll Need

9 inches pale blue paper twist, 3½ inches wide • 21 inches patterned paper twist, 3½ inches wide • Tape measure or yardstick • Scissors • Hot glue gun, glue sticks • 1-inch-diameter wooden angel head • Wood wool • 5 feet off-white satin ribbon, ⅛ inch wide • 26 inches pale blue satin ribbon, ⅛ inch wide

1 Untwist and flatten all paper twist. Cut pale blue paper twist into three 3-inch pieces. Cut patterned paper twist into three 3-inch pieces and a 12-inch piece.

2 Run a thin line of glue along a 3-inch side of blue paper twist. With a second blue paper, place a 3-inch side on top of glue, creating a long rectangle.

3 Run a thin line of glue down an unglued 3-inch side of rectangle. Place other unglued edge of rectangle on top of glue, forming a tube.

4 Gather an end of tube. Glue gathered end, forming a cone. This is the underskirt.

5 To make overskirt, round off 2 corners of a 3-inch side of a patterned paper piece. Repeat with another piece.

6 Gather unrounded side of each patterned piece. Glue gathered ends of each patterned piece to top of underskirt, overlapping top edges.

7 Run a thin line of glue down both 3½-inch sides of third piece of blue paper. Place third 3-inch pattern piece of paper on top of blue paper, pattern side up. This is the blouse.

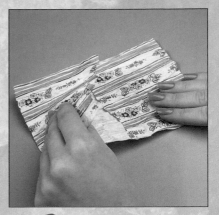

13 Mold a 2-inch-diameter clump of wood wool into a hair shape.

8 Fold the blouse in half, bringing glued sides together with patterned piece on top.

9 Gather glued sides together, and glue.

10 Glue bottom of blouse to top of skirt. Hold in place until glue sets.

11 Pull blue paper of shoulders out farther than patterned paper.

12 Glue angel's head on blouse, centering head between shoulders.

14 Glue wood hair to top of head.

15 Cut off-white ribbon into three 18-inch lengths and a 6-inch length. Cut pale blue ribbon into an 18-inch length and an 8-inch length.

16 Tie two 18-inch lengths of off-white around waist, making a bow at front of angel. Place a drop of glue on ribbon at back of waist to hold in place.

17 To make wings, fold 12-inch length of pattern paper in half and unfold. Run a thin line of glue just to right of center line.

18 Fold in right side to glue line. Run another thin line of glue just to left of center line. Fold in left side to glue line. Let glue dry.

19 Gather paper together at center line, forming wings.

20 Glue wings to center back of blouse.

21 Overlap remaining 18-inch length of off-white ribbon with 18-inch-length of pale blue ribbon. Make a 1-inch-diameter loopy bow. Tie off bow with 6-inch length of off-white ribbon. (See page 5 for instructions on making a loopy bow.)

22 Glue bow to top of hair.

23 Fold 8-inch length of pale blue ribbon in half. Glue ends to base of bow for a hanger.

Beaded Wreath

What You'll Need

3-inch bleached grapevine wreath • 22-inch string mauve beads, 3mm • 22-inch string blue beads, 3mm • Hot glue gun, glue sticks • 30 inches blue satin ribbon, $\frac{1}{16}$ inch wide • 36 inches mauve satin ribbon, $\frac{1}{16}$ inch wide • Tape measure or yardstick • Scissors • 3 blue ribbon roses, $\frac{1}{4}$ inch each • 2 rose leaves, $\frac{1}{2}$ inch each • Wire cutters

1 Glue an end of both bead strings to rear of wreath.

2 Wrap strings of beads around wreath. Finish by gluing ends of both strings to rear of wreath where strings were first glued.

3 Cut blue ribbon into an 18-inch length and a 12-inch length. Cut mauve ribbon into two 18-inch lengths. Overlap all 18-inch lengths of ribbon, and make a 2-inch bow. Glue bow to wreath; this is the wreath top.

4 Clip stems from roses and leaves. Glue them to lower right side of wreath between beads.

5 Fold 12-inch length of blue ribbon in half, and tie an overhand knot near open ends. Glue folded end just behind bow, making a hanger.

Tips and Variations

- Place narrow lace under beads for a pretty touch.
- Fabric stores stock special trims for holiday seasons. Look through seasonal bins for a special trim that strikes your fancy.
- Choose a color combination that matches your bedroom, and hang this ornament on the wall after your tree comes down.

O Christmas Tree!

What You'll Need

Scissors • Two 6×6-inch squares green pattern material • Pen or pencil • 6×6-inch square polyester batting • Pins • Sewing machine • Thread to match green material • 1 yard mini garland • Needle • Craft glue • 4 wood mini ornaments • 4 gold mini ornaments, 8mm each • 3 gold mini ornaments, 6mm each • 11 red bows, ⅜ inch each • 9 inches red satin ribbon, ¹⁄₁₆ inch wide • 12 inches red satin ribbon, ¼ inch wide

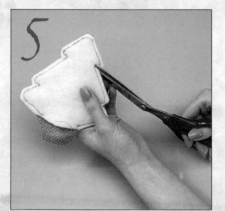

1 Copy and cut out pattern on page 64. (See page 5 for directions on cutting out patterns.)

2 Place pattern on the wrong side of green doubled material, and trace. Cut out tree. Cut out 1 batting tree.

3 Place material right sides together, and place batting tree on top. Pin together.

4 Sew pieces together with a ¼-inch seam allowance; leave an opening at base of tree to turn. Sew again to reinforce seams.

5 Trim seams, and clip curves. Turn tree right-side out. Sew opening shut.

6 Baste garland to tree at seams. (If you have garland left, apply a spot of glue to knot at end of nylon line and attach to back of tree.)

7 Randomly sew ornaments to tree. Glue ⅜-inch bows above ornaments to cover thread.

8 Fold 9-inch length of red ribbon in half. Glue ends to back of treetop.

9 Make a 1¼-inch bow from 12-inch length of red ribbon. Glue to top of tree.

Button-Down Santa

What You'll Need

12×12-inch squares material: red felt, black felt, muslin, burlap • Scissors • Pins • Thread: red, black, off-white, beige • Sewing machine • Polyester fiberfill • Needle • Extra-strong thread: 2 spools cream, 1 spool black • 70 or more buttons; 2 holes, various colors (white, off-white, black, red) and sizes (mostly ⅜ inch, some ¾ inch) • Permanent markers: black, red • Jute twine • Pencil • Embroidery thread: red, blue • Craft glue

1 Copy and cut out patterns on pages 62–63. (See page 5 for directions on cutting out patterns.)

2 Double all fabrics. Place suit and hat patterns on red felt. Cut out 2 suits, 2 hats, and 2 hatbands. Place boot pattern on black felt. Cut out 2 boots. Repeat to make 2 more boots. Place body pattern on muslin, and cut out 2 bodies. Cut an 8×3½-inch strip from burlap.

3 On a suit piece, fold felt along fold lines and A lines as shown on pattern at lower edges. Pin in place. Repeat for other suit piece.

4 Using red thread, sew along line A on all pinned corners.

5 Pin red suit together, with darts on outside. Sew suit along B lines, leaving sleeves and neck open.

6 Clip corners, and turn suit right side out. Stuff suit three-quarters full with fiberfill.

7 Using matching thread, sew body pieces along sewing lines, leaving bottom edge open.

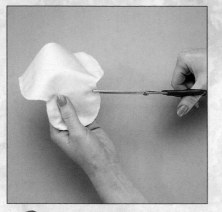

8 Clip curves, and turn body right side out. Stuff body with fiberfill. Baste lower edges shut.

9 Place Santa's body into suit.

10 Thread needle with extra-strong cream thread, doubled. Sew a running stitch about 3/16 inch from neck edge of Santa's suit. Pull thread to gather suit neck around body. Tie off thread, and trim excess.

11 Sew a hatband to lower edge of hat piece. Repeat with other hatband and hat piece.

12 Place hat pieces together with seams on inside, and sew only hatbands together.

13 Turn hat so seams are on outside, and sew hats together. Turn hat. Turn hatband up at seam.

14 Thread needle with extra-strong cream thread, and tie a knot 1/4 inch from end of thread. Insert needle through hatband, and knot thread at hatband. Clip thread 1/4 inch from knot. Repeat this all around hatband with cream and extra-strong black thread until hatband is filled with thread.

15 To make tassel, thread needle with extra-strong cream thread. Repeat procedure for hatband knots, but leave thread ends for tassel about 1 1/2 inches long. Repeat, using cream thread only, until tassel is full.

16 Sew 2 boots together on sewing lines indicated on pattern. Leave top of boot open. Repeat with other 2 boots.

17 Clip curves, and turn boots right side out. Stuff boots with polyester fiberfill.

18 Use extra-strong black thread to make a running stitch about 3/16 inch from upper edge of boot. Pull thread to gather boot shut. Tie off thread, and trim excess.

19 Thread needle with about 20 inches extra-strong cream thread, doubled. Insert needle into side of a boot and up through gathered center. Starting with a 3/4-inch button to cover boot top, thread on buttons for legs. Place a 3/4-inch red button about 1 1/4 inches up stack.

20 When button stack measures about 2 1/2 inches, insert needle into bottom of Santa's body, about 1/2 inch in from side. Bring needle back out about 1/4 inch away from where needle was inserted.

21 Take thread back down stack of buttons through second holes. Insert needle down through gathered center and out side of boot, just below gathering. Allow a little "give" on thread so you can add a jute bow later. Knot thread, and clip excess. Use black marker to color thread that shows around top of boot. Repeat for other leg.

22 Fold burlap in half, bringing 3 1/2-inch sides together.

23 Using matching thread, sew sides together, leaving top of sack open. Turn sack right-side out, and stuff about three-quarters full with fiberfill.

24 Cut jute into the following lengths: 15 inch, two 7 inch, and 24 inch.

25 Gather top of the sack about 1 inch down from opening. Wrap 15-inch length of twine around the gathering, and tie a bow.

26 Thread needle with about 20 inches of extra-strong cream thread, doubled. Insert needle into end of sleeve about 3/16 inch from edge. Make a running stitch around sleeve cuff. Pull thread to gather. Tie off thread, but do not cut it.

27 Begin threading buttons for arms. Start with a 3/4-inch white button, and follow with a 3/4-inch red button.

28 When about 1 inch of buttons have been threaded, insert needle through gathered area of Santa's sack and out other side. String buttons in reverse order for Santa's other arm (buttons on other side of sack are Santa's other arm).

29 Insert needle into other sleeve end about ³/₁₆ inch from edge. Make a running stitch around sleeve cuff. Pull thread to gather. Tie off thread, but do not cut it.

30 Insert needle back through second holes in buttons, through sack, and through second group of buttons.

31 Insert needle through gathered material at sleeve cuff and out below gathering. Knot thread, and clip excess. Use red marker to color thread that shows around sleeves.

32 With pencil, lightly draw Santa's lower lip and eyes as indicated on pattern.

33 Use red embroidery thread to satin stitch Santa's lower lip. Use blue embroidery thread to stitch French knots for Santa's eyes.

34 To make Santa's hair, moustache, and beard, thread needle with extra-strong cream thread. Insert needle into Santa's head and take a ¼-inch stitch, leaving about 2 inches hanging free on either side of stitch. (Do not tie knots.)

35 Repeat until hair and beard are thick. When finished, trim thread to shape hair and beard. For moustache, trim hanging ends to ½ inch.

36 Place glue on inside rim of Santa's hat. Place hat on Santa's head, with seams to sides. Hold until glue sets.

37 Tie 7-inch lengths of jute twine above bottom button on each leg to make bows.

38 Tie 24-inch length of jute twine around hat below tassel to make a bow. Trim ends to 2 inches. Spot glue twine in place on back of hat. Let dry.

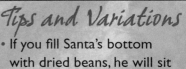

Tips and Variations
• If you fill Santa's bottom with dried beans, he will sit on your mantel.

21

Western Theme Tree

Put a new and different spin on your Christmas celebration by creating a Western theme for your tree. Decorate your tree with unique ornaments that say the American West: bandannas, cowboys, longhorn steers, and more. You can complete your Western tree with pointers on garlands, toppers, and skirts from the Introduction.

Holly Badge

What You'll Need

Paintbrushes: ½-inch, 5/0 • 5-pointed wood star, 2 inch • Acrylic paint: yellow, black • 2 holly leaves with berry, ½-inch leaves • Wire cutters • Hot glue gun, glue sticks • 2 inches red satin ribbon, ⅛ inch wide • 8 inches gold elastic cord

1 Using ½-inch brush, paint both sides and edges of star yellow.

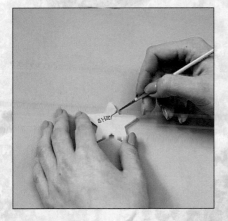

2 Using 5/0 brush, paint "Sheriff" in black.

3 Trim stems from holly leaves and berry. Glue leaves and berry on lower right of star.

4 Make a ¾-inch bow from ribbon. Glue bow above holly leaves.

5 Fold gold cord in half. Tie an overhand knot near open ends. Glue knot to back of star's top point.

Tips and Variations

There are stars of many shapes; you don't have to use a 5-pointed star. Sheriff badges came in many shapes and sizes. There were also U.S. Marshals and Texas Rangers in the old West; make a whole collection of badges!

Texas Santa

What You'll Need

Scissors • Felt squares: red, white, black, gold •
Pen or pencil • Chalk • Craft glue • Polyester
batting • 2 holly leaves with berry, ½-inch
leaves • Wire cutters • Hot glue gun, glue
sticks • Gold thread • Needle

1 Copy and cut out patterns
on page 61. (See page 5
for directions on cutting out
patterns.) On red felt, place
main figure and lips; on white,
place chaps, cuffs, beard, hatband, and hat pom-pom; on
black, place belt; on gold, place
belt buckle. Trace patterns on
felt with pen or pencil (use
chalk for black felt). Cut out all
patterns.

2 The sides showing lines
are the wrong sides.

3 Use craft glue to glue
pieces in place in the
following order: hat pom-
pom, hatband, beard, lips, belt,
belt buckle, chaps, and cuffs.
Let dry.

4 Place main figure pattern on black felt. Using
chalk, outline shape ½ inch
outside edges of pattern. Allow
extra space around legs for
chaps.

5 Cut out shape from
black felt.

6 Place main figure pattern
on batting. Trace shape
with a pen or pencil.

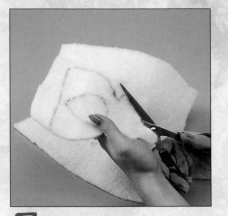

7 Cut out shape ¼ inch inside traced lines.

10 Pick up figure and batting, and place on black felt with batting in middle of felt pieces. If necessary, add more glue so all edges are glued to black felt. Let glue dry.

11 Trim black felt to within ⅛ inch of figure.

13 To make a hanger, double thread needle with gold thread. Draw needle through pom-pom.

14 Tie an overhand knot about 4 inches above figure. Cut off excess thread.

8 On wrong side of figure, run a thin line of craft glue around edges.

9 Place batting cutout on top of glue.

12 Trim stems from holly leaves and berry, and glue to hat with hot glue.

Tips and Variations

- Try tracing the pattern on ¼-inch-thick basswood, available at hobby shops. Then use a scroll saw to cut out the ornament. Paint the wood in your favorite colors with acrylic paints.
- Instead of glue, sew the figure to the black felt backing using a fancy stitch with a contrasting color thread.

On the Christmas Trail

What You'll Need

Wood horse, about 4×3½ inches • Acrylic paints: white, brown • ½-inch paintbrush • 13 inches red satin ribbon, ⅛ inch wide • Tape measure or yardstick • Scissors • 2-inch frosted sisal wreath • Craft glue • Tweezers • 7 jingle bells, 6mm each

1 Paint horse white. Let dry, and repaint to cover completely. Let dry. Paint pinto markings with brown paint. Let dry.

2 Cut ribbon into an 8-inch length and a 5-inch length.

3 For hanger, slip 8-inch length of ribbon through wreath and tie an overhand knot about ½ inch from open ends. Reshape wreath into an oval.

4 Slip wreath over horse's head, and place glue on mane where wreath hits. Hold wreath in place until glue sets. (Place ribbon in glue so horse hangs straight.)

5 Make a ¾-inch bow with 5-inch length of ribbon. Glue to right front side of wreath.

6 Using tweezers, glue jingle bells evenly around wreath.

Tips and Variations

• Paint the horse to match your favorite breed; an encyclopedia will have photographs of many breeds of horses. Painting the horse turquoise and pink will give your horse Southwestern style!

Pepper Yule Party

What You'll Need

12 plastic red peppers, ⅞ inch each • 26 inches red satin ribbon, ⅛ inch wide • 26 inches green satin ribbon, ⅛ inch wide • Tape measure or yardstick • Scissors • Hot glue gun, glue sticks

1 Braid ends of 3 peppers together.

2 Keep adding a pepper each time you braid wires from first row of peppers. This is a bit like making a French braid. Continue adding peppers.

3 After all 12 peppers have been braided, continue braiding wires together. Bend braided wire behind peppers to form a hook.

4 Cut both red and green ribbons into 18-inch lengths and 8-inch lengths.

5 Overlap 18-inch lengths of red and green ribbon, and make a 3-inch bow. Glue bow to top of peppers.

6 Insert red and green 8-inch lengths of ribbon through braided wire hook. Tie an overhand knot 1 inch from open ends for a hanger.

Tips and Variations

- Make a spicy arrangement for your front door by using larger red peppers.

- In many European countries, it is traditional to hang fruit and sometimes vegetables on a Christmas tree. You can do the same thing using miniature fruits and vegetables. Just be sure there are wires to braid.

- If the red coating on the peppers chips, red fingernail polish works as a great touch-up.

27

Christmas Kerchief

What You'll Need

Red bandanna • Iron, ironing board • 2 holly picks with 3 leaves, ¾-inch leaves • Hot glue gun, glue sticks • 8 gold mini pinecones on picks • 8 inches red satin ribbon, ⅛ inch wide • Red thread • Needle

1 Iron bandanna. Fold and iron plain border under so only patterned area shows.

2 Fold bandanna, matching opposite corners, into a triangle. Iron flat.

3 Fold long edge down ½ inch. Continue folding in same direction until about 2 inches remain unfolded at tip of bandanna.

4 Fold bandanna in half, with tip as center. Tie a knot in center; do not pull knot too tightly.

5 Tie a square knot about 4 inches from ends of bandanna, leaving a hole in middle. Iron ends flat.

6 Insert a holly pick into each side of last knot made. Place a dab of hot glue into each side to hold holly in place.

7 Arrange pinecones into 2 groups of 4. Apply hot glue to stems of first group, and place it into sides of knot with holly. Repeat for other group and side.

8 Fold ribbon in half, and tie an overhand knot near open ends. Sew folded end to back of square knot.

Tips and Variations

• Bandannas come in many fun colors. A turquoise or pink bandanna will make a Southwestern-style ornament.

Festive Bolo

What You'll Need

21 inches black leather, ⅛ inch wide •
Scissors • Tape measure or yardstick •
2-inch bolo

1 Cut leather into a 20-inch length and a 1-inch length. Fold 20-inch length of leather in half. Make sure colored side of leather is face up.

2 Starting at top rear of bolo, thread about 3½ inches of ends of leather through openings in bolo.

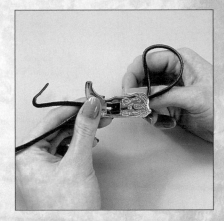

3 Again starting at top rear of bolo, thread 1-inch length of leather into bolo openings between strands of 20-inch piece. This is to keep leather from slipping in bolo opening. Trim excess leather at top or bottom of bolo.

Tips and Variations

• Bolos come in many different metals and shapes. When choosing additional shapes, be sure the leather will feed through the bolo's holes.

Cowgirl Hat

What You'll Need

12 inches tricolor cord, 4mm wide • 4-inch white felt Stetson hat • Hot glue gun, glue sticks • Scissors • 14 rhinestone settings, 4mm • 7 green rhinestones, 4mm each • 7 red rhinestones, 4mm each • Orange stick • 8 inches gold elastic cord

1 Tie tricolor cord around brim of hat, with knot at side of hat. Place a dab of hot glue at both sides of hat to secure cord to hat.

2 Trim ends of cord so they overhang hat brim by ⅛ inch. Glue ends to hat brim to secure.

3 Push points of a rhinestone setting through hat brim from underneath to top. Place a rhinestone into points.

4 Using orange stick, push points over rhinestone to hold it in place. Repeat until all rhinestones have been placed around brim, alternating green and red rhinestones.

5 Fold elastic cord in half, and tie an overhand knot about 1 inch from open ends. Glue knot to bottom front edge of brim.

Tips and Variations

• For variety, use miniature felt cowboy/cowgirl hats in different colors or shapes. You can also vary the look by choosing studs other than rhinestones. Instead of tricolor cord, glue lace around the brim for a more feminine look.

Red-Hot Wreath

What You'll Need

13 inches green satin ribbon, ⅛ inch wide •
Tape measure or yardstick • Scissors • 3 plastic
red peppers, ⅞ inch each • Wire cutters • 3-inch-
diameter grapevine wreath • Hot glue gun,
glue sticks

1 Cut ribbon into a 3-inch
length and a 10-inch
length. Make a bow from
3-inch length of ribbon.

2 Trim stems from red
peppers. Glue in place
on wreath.

3 Glue bow just above
peppers.

4 Insert 10-inch length of
ribbon through center
of wreath for a hanger. Match
ribbon ends, then put a dab of
glue on top rear of wreath to
secure ribbon in place. Tie an
overhand knot 3 inches above
wreath. Make a bow above
overhand knot on hanger.

Jolly Clay Santa

What You'll Need

Bakeable plastic clay: beige, red, white • Tooth-picks • Paring knife • Paper clip • Wire cutters • Rolling pin • Acrylic paint: white, blue • Paint-brushes: 5/0, ½ inch • Baking sheet • Spatula • Water-based gloss varnish • 8 inches white satin ribbon, ⅛ inch wide

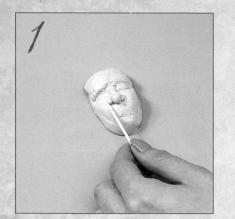

1 Make a 2-inch egg shape for Santa's head with beige clay; flatten back of egg. Add small balls and "snakes" of clay to build up forehead, nose, cheeks, and eyes. Use tooth-picks as well as your fingers to place balls and snakes; use paring knife to refine face.

2 Snip off small end of a paper clip; push half of U into back of Santa's head for a hanger.

3 Roll a small snake, about ⅜ inches long, from red clay. Shape into an arc, and place on Santa's face for a lower lip.

4 Roll about 25 snakes from white clay. Press an end of each snake onto face to form beard. Taper beard ends with fingertips.

5 Roll 4 larger snakes from white clay for eyebrows and mustache. One end of each should taper. Place 2 above eyes and 2 above lip.

6 Use rolling pin to roll red clay to about ⅛-inch thickness. Use paring knife to cut a 2⅔×4-inch triangle for Santa's hat.

7 Place base of triangle across Santa's forehead. Pull tip of triangle down around side of base.

8 Make about 34 balls of several different sizes from white clay. Press them in a random arrangement along the bottom ½ inch of hat's base to form white hat cuff.

9 Make several more balls from white clay. Press these on tip of Santa's hat.

10 Paint Santa's eyes white using the 5/0 brush and white paint. Let dry Mix a small amount of white and blue paint to create light blue. Paint iris of Santa's eyes light blue. Let dry. Paint Santa's pupils dark blue, using only blue paint.

11 Move ornament to a baking sheet with a spatula. Bake at 200°F for 2 hours. Let cool.

12 Use ½-inch brush to paint ornament with varnish. Let dry 24 hours.

13 Thread 8-inch length of white ribbon through paper clip on back. Tie an overhand knot near open ends.

Tips and Variations

- You can make many Christmas ornaments from plastic clay; let your imagination run wild.

- A low temperature and long baking time were used because Santa's head has a lot of white and the egg shape is thick. Don't hurry the baking process by turning the oven to a higher temperature; this will cause scorching and burning. Generally, the longer the clay is baked, the stronger it will be.

Angel of the Vine

What You'll Need

10 inches iridescent paper twist, 3½ inches wide • Tape measure or yardstick • Scissors • Hot glue gun, glue sticks • 5-inch gold grape spray • ⅝-inch-diameter wood doll head (with drilled hole) • Wood wool • 3 holly leaves, 1½ inches each • Wire cutters • 18 inches gold-edged white ribbon, ½ inch wide • 8 inches white satin ribbon, ⅛ inch wide

1 Open and flatten paper twist. Cut paper twist into two 5-inch lengths. Fold each piece in half, bringing 3½-inch sides together.

2 With 1 folded paper twist, gather open ends together and glue. Repeat for other folded paper twist. These are angel's wings.

3 Glue gathered ends of wings to back of grape spray stem.

4 Place head on grape stem so it sits on top of wings. Glue head in place. Some stem will protrude above head; turn this piece back to form a small loop for a hanger.

5 Compress about a 1-inch-diameter clump of wood wool. Glue wood wool to top of angel's head. Arrange wood wool around grape stem to hide it.

6 Clip stems from holly leaves. Glue leaves under angel's chin.

7 Make a bow from 18-inch length of ribbon. Glue bow under angel's chin on top of holly leaves.

8 Slip an end of 8-inch length of ribbon through loop made from stem. Fold ribbon in half, and tie an overhand knot ½ inch from open ends.

Dove of Peace

What You'll Need

1 sheet white paper, 80 pound • Scissors • Pencil • Craft knife • Pin • Rubber cement • 20 inches burgundy satin ribbon with picot edges, ¼ inch wide • Tape measure or yard-stick • Hot glue gun, glue sticks

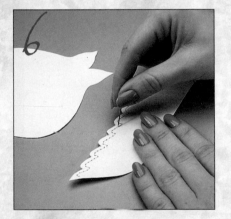

1 Copy and cut out patterns on page 63. (See page 5 for directions on cutting out patterns.)

2 Trace patterns on paper.

3 Cut out bird and wings with scissors and craft knife.

4 Slice slits for wings where noted on pattern with craft knife.

5 On back of paper, draw a line that follows the outline of wings and tail about ⅛ inch in from edge.

6 Following lines, poke a pinhole through paper every ⅛ inch.

7 Fold ½ inch of front of bird's head together, matching beaks. Glue head together with rubber cement.

8 Poke a pinhole through the paper at eye mark where indicated on pattern.

9 Slide wings through slits, and center them.

10 Cut ribbon into an 8-inch length and a 12-inch length. Fold 8-inch length of ribbon in half. Glue open ends to bird's body above shoulders where indicated on pattern for a hanger.

11 Make a 1-inch bow from 12-inch length of ribbon. Glue bow over ends of 8-inch length of ribbon.

Children's Theme Tree

Your young ones will absolutely love the clever ornaments you make to decorate a theme tree just for children. Dinosaurs, teddy bears, and snowmen will prance about your tree on Christmas morning. Be sure to see the Introduction for some great suggestions for children's tree skirts, garlands, and toppers.

Pom-Pom Snowman

What You'll Need

Pom-poms: 2½ inch, 2 inch, 1 inch • Hot glue gun, glue sticks • ⅝-inch top hat • 3½-inch broom • 8-inch striped knit scarf, ⅞ inch wide • ½-inch plastic carrot • Wire cutters • 2 wiggle eyes, 4mm each • 3 black beads, 4mm each • Craft glue • Tweezers • 8 inches white satin ribbon, ⅛ inch wide

1 Find center of 2½-inch and 2-inch poms, and glue centers together with hot glue. Attach 1-inch pom to 2-inch pom-pom in same way, forming a snowman.

2 Hot glue top hat to top of 1-inch pom.

3 Lay broom diagonally across snowman, and hot glue upper end of broom to hat's brim.

4 Hot glue lower part of broom to bottom pom.

5 Tie scarf around snowman's neck, with knot at side opposite broom.

6 Snip off tip of carrot. Hot glue tip to top pom for nose.

7 With craft glue and tweezers, glue wiggle eyes in place. Glue beads on second pom for buttons. Let dry.

8 Fold ribbon in half; make an overhand knot ½ inch from open ends. Hot glue folded end to back of hat.

Dinosaur in December

What You'll Need

Felt squares: bright blue, bright yellow • Scissors • Pen or pencil • Polyester batting • Craft glue • 6mm wiggle eye • 10 inches gold thread • Needle

1 Copy and cut out pattern on page 61. (See page 5 for directions on cutting out patterns.)

2 Trace pattern on blue felt with a pen or pencil.

3 Following traced lines, cut out figure. The side with traced lines is wrong side.

4 Place pattern on bright yellow felt, and trace a general shape at least ½ inch outside figure.

5 Cut out shape for backing.

6 Unfold 1 thickness of batting, and trace main figure on it.

7 Redraw pattern ¼ inch inside the traced line.

8 Cut out figure, following inner traced line.

12 Cut out different-size triangular shapes from yellow felt for trim.

9 Place batting on top of wrong side of blue felt. Run a thin line of craft glue at edge of figure, being sure that some glue is placed under outside edge of batting.

13 Fold triangles in half, and cut a nip out of bottom of triangles. Open flat.

16 To make a hanger, thread needle with gold thread. Draw needle through dinosaur's spine (through both pieces of felt) just below blue edge.

17 For a hanger, tie an overhand knot about 4 inches above figure. Cut off excess thread.

10 Place figure and batting on top of right side of yellow felt backing. Press glued edges of blue felt onto backing. Let dry (about 20 minutes).

11 Trim backing material to ⅛ inch of figure, except at spine. Scallop spine edge, leaving about ½ inch of material.

14 Randomly glue triangles to dinosaur's front.

15 Glue wiggle eye in place.

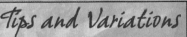

Tips and Variations

• Trace the pattern on a ¼-inch-thick piece of basswood; use a scroll saw to cut out the figure. Decorate with acrylic paints.

• Instead of glue, use a fancy stitch on your sewing machine in a contrasting color to sew the figure to the backing.

Bears on a Sleigh Ride

What You'll Need

4½-inch sleigh • Red enamel paint • Red oak stain • ½-inch paintbrush • 11 assorted bears: different colors and sizes (between ¾ and 1¾ inches) • Hot glue gun, glue sticks • 5 candy canes, ⅝ inch each • 15 inches tricolor cord, 4mm • Tape measure or yardstick • Scissors • 2 holly leaves and berry, ½ inch leaves • Wire cutters • 2 inches red satin ribbon, ⅛ inch • 1-inch sisal wreath • Craft glue • Frosted glitter

1 Paint carriage section (inside, outside, and underneath) of sleigh red. Stain runners with oak stain.

2 Starting at rear of sleigh, hot glue bears in place. Glue smallest bears wherever there is a hole in bear arrangement. Hot glue a candy cane to the paws of 5 bears.

3 Cut tricolor cord into a 10-inch length and a 5-inch length. Sear ends of cords to prevent unraveling.

4 Hot glue an end of 10-inch length of cord to sleigh's front; hot glue other end to rear of sleigh.

5 Make a 2-inch bow from 5-inch length of cord. Hot glue bow to sleigh's front to cover end of 10-inch length of cord.

6 Trim stems from holly leaves and berry, and hot glue them above bow.

7 Make a 1-inch bow from red ribbon. If the wreath has a bow, remove it. In its place, attach the 1-inch bow using hot glue.

8 Spot glue wreath to rear of sleigh to cover end of 10-inch length of cord.

9 Using your finger, spread glue over tops of runners, top edge of sleigh, tops of bears' heads, and top of wreath. Sprinkle on frosted glitter. Let dry.

Christmas Olé

What You'll Need

4-inch sombrero • 8 inches tricolor cord, 3mm • Hot glue gun, glue sticks • Wire cutters • ¾-inch glazed holly leaf pick • 2 red berries, ⅛ inch each • 6mm jingle bell • 3 plaid stockings, 1½ inches each • 3 Santa hats, ¾ inch each • 8 inches gold elastic cord

1 Wrap tricolor cord around base of hat's crown. Spot glue in place.

2 Trim ends of cord at an angle. Apply a dab of glue to each end to prevent unraveling. Glue ends to edge of brim.

3 Take apart holly pick, and trim stems from leaves. Glue leaves in place where cord overlaps at crown's base.

4 Glue a berry onto each holly leaf. Glue bell where cord overlaps at crown's base.

5 Turn hat over. Alternate Santa plaid stockings and hats at edge of hat's brim, spacing evenly. Hot glue in place.

6 Turn hat upright. To make a hanger, fold gold cord in half, and tie an overhand knot ½ inch from open ends. Glue folded end to top center of crown.

Noel Rocking Horse

What You'll Need

3-inch embroidery frame • Walnut stain • Paintbrushes: ½ inch, 5/0 • 5×5-inch square muslin • Scissors • 10 inches green eyelet, ½ inch wide • Hot glue gun, glue sticks • 13 inches red satin picot-edged ribbon, ¼ inch wide • Tape measure or yardstick • 3-inch rocking horse • Acrylic paint: white, red, green, yellow

1 Stain embroidery frame using ½-inch paintbrush.

2 Place muslin in frame, pulling fabric tight. Trim excess material.

3 Glue eyelet to back of frame, overlapping ends.

 Cut ribbon into a 5-inch length and an 8-inch length. Make a 1-inch bow from 5-inch length of ribbon. Glue bow to frame at metal hardware.

5 Insert 8-inch length of ribbon through metal hardware gap. Tie an overhand knot ½ inch from open ends for a hanger.

6 Paint horse's mane white with ½-inch brush. Let dry. Paint horse's body red. Let dry. (For steps 6–9, if needed for full coverage, paint a second coat.)

7 Paint rocker and saddle green. Let dry. (Horse's ears and tips of rocker will overhang frame, so paint back of horse in these areas. Paint all edges of horse.) Paint mane yellow. Let dry.

8 Using 5/0 brush, add yellow trim to rocker and saddle areas. Paint a green bow and braid to mane and an eyelid and eyelashes to face.

9 Glue horse to muslin.

And a Partridge in a ...

What You'll Need

2-inch partridge • Wire cutters • 2½-inch bark nest • Hot glue gun, glue sticks • 38 inches red satin picot-edged ribbon, ¼ inch wide • Tape measure or yardstick • Scissors • Moss

1 Snip wire from bird's feet. Glue bird into opening of nest.

2 Cut ribbon into following lengths: 8 inch, 24 inch, and 6 inch. Thread 8-inch length of ribbon through hook at top of nest. Tie an overhand knot ½ inch from ends for a hanger.

3 Arrange and glue moss around hook and ribbon.

4 Make a 2½-inch loopy bow from 24-inch length of ribbon. Tie off bow with 6-inch length of ribbon. (See page 5 for instructions on making a loopy bow.)

5 Glue bow to moss in front of hook.

Tips and Variations

- Instead of moss, sprinkle on crystal glitter for a snow-covered look.
- Try a different type of bird: cardinal, blue jay, robin, or any other bird that strikes your fancy.

Santa's Sleigh

What You'll Need

4-inch wicker sleigh • 3 gift packages, ¾ inch each • 2 gift packages, ½ inch each • Hot glue gun, glue sticks • 3 inches red satin ribbon, ⅛ inch wide • 1½-inch sisal wreath • 2 candy canes, 2¾ inches each • 16 inches gold elastic cord • Tape measure or yardstick • Scissors

1 Glue ¾-inch packages into sleigh, keeping packages to front of sleigh.

2 Glue ½-inch packages into sleigh, keeping packages to front of sleigh.

3 Make a ¾-inch bow from red ribbon.

4 If wreath came with a bow, remove it. Glue ¾-inch bow in its place. Set wreath aside.

5 Glue candy canes into left rear corner of sleigh.

6 Glue wreath in front of candy canes.

7 Cut gold cord into an 8-inch length and two 4-inch lengths. Glue an end of 8-inch length to front of sleigh; glue other end to rear of sleigh.

8 Make two 1-inch bows from the 4-inch lengths of gold cord. Glue a bow at each end of 8-inch length of gold cord.

Tips and Variations

• Instead of gift packages, fill the sleigh with candy, bears, small flowers, miniature sports equipment, or a special gift such as an engagement ring.

44

Braided Candy Cane

What You'll Need

2 pieces red calico, 1½×13 inches each • White material with red dots, 1½×13 inches • Iron, ironing board • 3 lengths covered florist wire, 18 inches each • Hot glue gun, glue sticks • Wire cutters • Scissors • 16 inches red satin ribbon, ⅛ inch wide • 16 inches white satin ribbon, ⅛ inch wide

5 Overlay second red and white ribbon lengths, and make a 1½-inch bow. Glue bow over hanger ends.

1 Turn up 1 long edge of a calico strip ¼ inch. Iron flat. Place a length of florist wire into fold. Roll fabric around wire. Spot glue edges in place. Clip florist wire that sticks out from strip. Repeat with other 2 strips of material.

2 Braid three strips together.

3 Turn ends back on themselves, and glue in place. Cut off extra material. Bend into a candy cane shape.

4 Cut red and white ribbon into two 8-inch lengths. Overlay a length of red and white ribbon. Fold in half, and glue ends together. Glue ends to top edge of candy cane for hanger.

Tips and Variations

• You can use this same technique to make a wreath. Use strips that are 18 inches long. After braiding, turn only one end back on itself. Shape the weaving into a circle, and glue the unfinished end behind the wreath. Glue 1-inch eyelet around the outside edge of the wreath.

Yuletide Bauble

What You'll Need

15 inches tricolor rattail cord, 3mm • 4 feet 10 inches gold rattail cord, 2mm • 4 feet red satin rattail cord, 2mm • Tape measure or yardstick • Scissors • Craft glue • 1 spray red carnations, 1 inch flowers • Wire cutters • Hot glue gun, glue sticks • 2 sprays gold balls, 3mm • Florist tape • 2-piece clear plastic egg, 4 inches • 23-inch string gold beads, 2mm • 18 gold balls, 9.5mm each • 8 gold balls, 12mm each

1 Cut tricolor cord into 10½-inch length and 4½-inch length. Cut gold cord into 3-foot length, 1-foot length, and 10-inch length. Cut red cord into 3-foot length and 1-foot length. Sear ends of tricolor cord to prevent unraveling. Apply a dab of craft glue to ends of gold and red cord lengths to prevent unraveling.

2 Trim bottoms from 3 carnations; arrange them in a circle. Hot glue carnation ends together.

3 Arrange remaining carnations in a 2½-inch-high spray. Insert a gold ball spray on either side; bind stems together with florist tape. Trim stems.

4 Trim bottoms of carnation leaves to 1½ inches long. Arrange leaves around bottom of carnation spray, and hot glue in place.

5 Insert carnation and leaf spray into center of 3-carnation arrangement. Hot glue in place.

6 Open plastic egg, and center carnation arrangement in bottom of egg half with inner edge. Hot glue spray in place. Close egg.

7 Fold 10½-inch tricolor cord in half. Hot glue middle of cord to bottom of egg, covering seam. Hot glue cord up either side of egg, covering seam. (The cord will not reach to egg top.)

8 Hot glue an end of bead string to an end of tricolor cord near egg top. Make loops with bead string, with 2 longer loops and then 2 shorter loops. Glue loop ends to tricolor cord.

9 Hot glue 4½-inch tricolor cord around egg top, touching but not covering ends of tricolor cord covering egg seam.

10 Hot glue 12mm balls above 4½-inch tricolor cord.

11 Hot glue 9.5mm balls to cover spaces between larger balls.

12 Make a 1-inch loopy bow from 3-foot lengths of gold and red cord. Use 1-foot lengths of gold and red cord to secure bow. (See page 5 for instructions on making a loopy bow.) Attach loopy bow to egg top with an overhand knot; hot glue in place. (Use 1-foot length of red cord that secured loopy bow to tie overhand knot.)

13 To make a hanger, insert 10-inch gold cord through a loop at egg top. Tie an overhand knot about ½ inch from open ends.

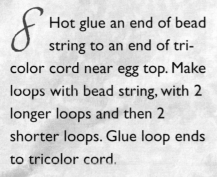

Tips and Variations

• Try different varieties and colors of flowers.

• Instead of flowers, create a scene using miniature elves or animals.

Country Theme Tree

Amid the hustle and bustle of city life, the call of the countryside is enticing. Reflect a simpler lifestyle with country ornaments such as Holiday Holstein and Old World St. Nick to make your hearth even warmer. Add an extra touch to your country tree by using the garland, skirt, and topper suggestions found in the Introduction.

Holiday Holstein

What You'll Need

4-inch wood cow • ½-inch paintbrush • Acrylic paint: white, black • ⅝-inch red wood heart • Hot glue gun, glue sticks • 15 inches red satin ribbon, ⅛ inch wide • Tape measure or yardstick • Scissors • ⅜-inch cowbell • 2 holly leaves with berry, ½-inch leaves

1 Paint cow with 2 coats of white paint. Let dry. Paint markings on cow with black paint.

2 Glue heart to side front of cow.

3 Cut ribbon into following lengths: 3 inch, 4 inch, and 8 inch. Thread bell onto 3-inch length. Place ribbon around cow's neck, and spot glue ribbon to back of neck.

4 Make a 1-inch bow from 4-inch ribbon length. Glue bow over ends of 3-inch length of ribbon on cow's neck.

5 Fold 8-inch ribbon length in half, and tie an overhand knot ½ inch from open ends. Glue ends to cow's back halfway along body for hanger.

6 Glue holly leaves and berry on front of cow, just in front of hanger.

Tips and Variations

• If you can't find a prepainted red heart, get an unpainted one and paint it with red enamel paint for a shiny surface.

• An encyclopedia will have photographs of many different breeds of cows; choose another breed for a different look.

Old World St. Nick

What You'll Need

9¾ inches red paper twist, 7 inches wide •
7 inches brown paper twist, 3½ inches wide •
Tape measure or yardstick • Scissors • Hot glue
gun, glue sticks • Pencil • 32 inches gold elastic
cord • Wood wool • ½-inch prewrapped present •
2 candy canes, 2 inches each • 2 holly leaves,
½-inch leaves • Wire cutters • ¼-inch jingle bell •
15mm wood bead

1 Open and flatten all paper twist. Cut red twist into the following lengths: 4 inch, 3 inch, and 2¾ inch.

2 With 4-inch red twist, fold up ½ inch on 7-inch side. Paper is now 3½×7 inches. This is Santa's body. The folded side will be on inside bottom of Santa.

3 Glue a 3½-inch end over other 3½-inch end, forming a tube (the ½-inch fold is on inside of tube).

4 Squeeze together unfolded end and glue, forming a 3½-inch-high cone.

5 Fold 3-inch red twist in half, forming a 3×3½-inch rectangle.

6 Make a pencil mark 1 inch from 3-inch side.

7 Cut an arc from pencil mark to other corner of 3-inch edge (cut through both thicknesses of paper).

8 Fold each top corner back ¼ inch to form cape lapels. Glue 1 lapel to top of cone that forms the body. Wrap cape around cone, and glue other lapel over first.

9 Gather top of cape to top of cone, and glue to cone.

10 Cut gold cord into following lengths: 8 inch, two 12 inch. Fold 8-inch cord in half. Make an overhand knot ½ inch from open ends. Put aside.

11 With 2¾-inch paper twist, fold ¾ inch up on the 7-inch side for cuff of hood. The paper is now 3×7 inches. The folded side will be on the outside front of hood.

12 With cuff on outside, fold hood in half.

13 Starting at fold and opposite cuff, cut an arc to edge of cuff on opposite side.

14 Insert tied gold cord into fold for a hanger.

15 Glue hood along cut edge, being sure to glue hanger also.

16 Fold brown paper twist in half, forming a 3½×3½-inch square; folded edge is bottom of sack.

17 At fold, make a pencil mark 1 inch in from each side. Make a pencil mark on each edge 2 inches down from top of sack.

18 Cut an arc from mark on fold to mark on edge. Repeat for other side. This is curved bottom of Santa's sack.

19 Glue sides together; let dry. Turn sack inside out.

20 Stuff bag with wood wool.

21 Gather sack 1 inch from top.

22 Glue present in opening of sack. Glue candy canes behind present.

23 Tie two 12-inch lengths of gold cord around gathered opening of sack. Tie a 1-inch bow at front of sack with cords.

24 Trim stems from holly leaves. Glue leaves just below bow.

25 Glue jingle bell where holly leaves meet. Set sack aside.

26 Glue wood bead on top of cone that forms body for Santa's head.

27 Place hood over head, and glue hood in place at neck back.

28 Roll a clump of wood wool, and form a beard around bottom of Santa's face. Glue in place.

29 With another clump of wood wool, make Santa's hair as you did his beard in step 28. Glue in place.

30 Glue hood to top of hair.

31 Glue sack, at an angle, to front of Santa.

Country Christmas Goose

What You'll Need

2¾-inch goose • 5¾ inches red satin ribbon, ¼ inch wide • 18 inches red satin ribbon, ⅛ inch wide • 19 inches red-checked cloth ribbon, ½ inch wide • Tape measure or yardstick • Scissors • Hot glue gun, glue sticks • 2½-inch hay bale • 2 holly leaves with 2 berries, ½-inch leaves • Wire cutters

1 This type of goose often comes with a felt bow on its neck. Carefully remove felt bow but leave felt neck band.

2 Cut ¼-inch ribbon into a ¾-inch length and a 5-inch length. Cut ⅛-inch ribbon into a 10-inch length, a 7-inch length, and a 1-inch length. Cut red-checked ribbon into a 7-inch length and a 12-inch length. Cover felt band with ¾-inch length of ¼-inch ribbon; glue in place.

3 To make a hanger, fold 10-inch length of ⅛-inch ribbon in half. Glue ends to goose's neck back on top of ribbon ends. Make a 1-inch bow with 5-inch length of ¼-inch ribbon. Glue bow to cover ribbon ends on back of neck.

4 Glue 7-inch length of red-checked ribbon around length of bale. Hot glue ends in place.

5 Wrap 7-inch length of ⅛-inch ribbon around bale, on top of checked ribbon. Glue ends in place.

6 Make a 3-inch bow from 12-inch length of red-checked ribbon. Wrap center knot of bow with 1-inch length of ⅛-inch ribbon. Glue bow to front of bale, covering glued ends of wrapped ribbons.

7 Trim stems from holly leaves. Glue leaves into bow knot on both sides. Trim berry stems, and glue onto holly leaves.

8 Clip wires protruding from goose's feet. Glue feet to top of bale, with goose turned slightly to side.

Buttons 'n' Eyelet Wreath

What You'll Need

8 inches eggshell satin ribbon, ⅛ inch wide • Hot glue gun, glue sticks • 4-inch grapevine wreath • 12 inches eggshell eyelet, 1 inch wide • 5 white buttons, ⅝ inch each • 20 white buttons, ⅜ inch each • Craft glue

1 Fold ⅛-inch ribbon in half. Tie an overhand knot ½ inch from open ends. Hot glue folded end to back of wreath.

3 Arrange ⅝-inch buttons around wreath in a random arrangement.

2 Hot glue eyelet to back of wreath, overlapping ends.

4 Arrange ⅜-inch buttons randomly around wreath. Glue buttons in place with craft glue.

Tips and Variations

• You don't need to buy new buttons; the ones you have collected over the years will be fine.

• For variety, use colored buttons and a complementary color eyelet.

Old-Fashioned Butter Mold

What You'll Need

12 inches blue-checked fabric ribbon, ½ inch wide • Hot glue gun, glue sticks • Heart-shape tin butter mold • 3-leaved glazed holly pick with berries, ½-inch leaves • Wire cutters • 2 inches blue-checked fabric ribbon, ⅛ inch wide • 8 inches gold elastic cord

1 Make a 2½-inch bow from ½-inch ribbon. Glue bow to top of butter mold.

2 Take apart holly pick, and clip stems. Glue leaves in knot of bow. Do the same with 2 berries.

3 Make a ¾-inch bow from ⅛-inch ribbon. Glue to bottom of butter mold.

4 To make a hanger, fold elastic cord in half. Tie an overhand knot ½ inch from open ends. Glue folded end of cord to back of 2½-inch bow.

Tips and Variations

• You can find tin butter molds in cake decorating or candy supply stores. Try a variety of shapes to make a whole series of ornaments.

Jute Twist

What You'll Need

2 red berry sprays, 3½ inches each • Hot glue gun, glue sticks • Jute twine • Tape measure or yardstick • Scissors

1 Bend both berry sprays into a C shape.

2 Glue stems of sprays together, with Cs facing each other.

3 Cut jute into the following lengths: 3 foot, two 10 inch, and 8 inch. Make a loopy bow from 3-foot length. Tie center of bow with both 10-inch lengths. (See page 5 for instructions on making a loopy bow.)

4 Glue bow to stems of sprays.

5 Fold 8-inch length of jute in half. Glue open ends to back of stems for a hanger.

Tips and Variations

• You can use any color berries you wish. Be sure the spray is three to four inches long; a larger spray may be too heavy for the tree limb.

Joy to the World

What You'll Need

2-inch square polyester batting • Scissors • 3-inch globe ornament • Hot glue gun, glue sticks • ¾-inch penguin • 2 sisal trees, 2 inches each

1 Cut a small hole in center of batting. Cut batting into an uneven circle.

3 Glue penguin just in front of hanger. Glue trees to either side of penguin.

2 Place batting on top of globe, with hanger in batting hole. Glue batting into place at North Pole.

Tips and Variations

• Instead of a penguin, use a picture of your child. Find a photograph of your child that is about 1½×2 inches. Using a craft knife, cut your child out from the rest of the photograph. Glue the outline to a thin piece of cardboard. Trim excess cardboard.

Bountiful Santa

What You'll Need

Felt squares: red, black • Scissors • Craft glue • Foam ball, 3-inch diameter • Sequin pins • Wood ball, 30mm diameter • Paintbrushes: $\frac{1}{2}$ inch, 5/0 liner • Acrylic paint: white, black, blue, red • White craft fur • 9 inches red satin ribbon, $\frac{1}{16}$ inch wide • $\frac{1}{4}$-inch white pom-pom • Hot glue gun, glue sticks • 2 holly leaves with berry, $\frac{1}{2}$-inch leaves • Wire cutters • 2 candy canes, $2\frac{1}{2}$ inches each • 10 inches plaid fabric ribbon, $\frac{3}{8}$ inch wide • Frosted sisal tree, $3\frac{1}{2}$ inches

1 Copy and cut out patterns on page 64. (See page 5 for instructions for cutting out patterns.)

2 Unless otherwise noted, use craft glue. Cut body pieces, arms, and hat from red felt. Place glue on foam ball. Attach body pieces to ball, and hold in place with pins; the pieces will overlap slightly. When glue dries, remove pins. Set aside.

3 Paint wood ball white with $\frac{1}{2}$-inch brush. Let dry.

4 From craft fur, cut 2-inch-diameter circle for bottom, $10 \times \frac{3}{4}$-inch piece for belt, two $1\frac{1}{2} \times \frac{1}{2}$-inch pieces for cuffs, $2\frac{1}{2} \times \frac{3}{4}$-inch piece for chest, $5 \times \frac{3}{4}$-inch piece for collar, $6 \times \frac{1}{2}$-inch piece for hat trim; cut out beard using pattern.

5 Cut mittens and belt buckle from black felt.

6 Place glue on a straight side of hat; overlap glued side to other straight side.

7 Glue hat trim to bottom edge of cone.

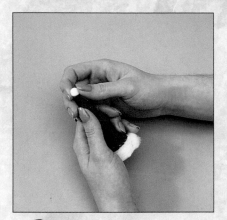

8 To make a hanger, fold red ribbon in half. Insert open ends into top of cone. Glue ends in place. Glue white pom-pom to top of hat. Set hat aside.

9 Glue mittens to straight ends of arms, and glue cuffs to tops of mittens.

10 Glue Santa together in following order: white circle to bottom of ball, belt around middle of ball, rounded ends of arms to either side of top of ball, chest piece from top of ball to belt, and belt buckle to center front of belt.

11 Hot glue wood ball to top of foam ball for head.

12 Wrap collar around neck, with ends meeting in middle of front. Spot glue in place.

13 Glue on Santa's beard.

14 Glue Santa's hat to head, with hat seam in back.

15 Using liner brush and paints, paint Santa's face as shown.

16 Trim stems from holly leaves and berry. Glue leaves and berry to Santa's beard beneath his right cheek.

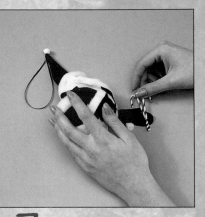

17 Cross candy canes, and hot glue them together. Hot glue crossed candy canes to Santa's right mitten.

18 Hot glue right mitten tip to Santa's buckle.

19 Make a 1¾-inch bow from plaid ribbon. Hot glue bow to stem of tree.

20 Hot glue tree to left side of Santa's belt buckle, and hot glue Santa's left mitten to tree base.

Cross-Stitch Christmas

What You'll Need

7×8-inch piece white Aida cloth, 14 count • 6-strand cotton embroidery floss (see color key) • #24 tapestry needle • Iron-on backing • 3×4-inch piece red felt • Scissors • 12 inches red satin ribbon, 1/8 inch wide • Tape measure or yardstick • Craft glue

1 Find center of cloth, and begin stitching there. Use 2 strands to stitch according to chart. For candy cane, make first stitch of cross-stitch in white and second stitch in red.

2 When all cross-stitching is done, backstitch around Santa's beard and fur with 1 strand of black. Backstitch around Rudolph's antlers, paws, and tail with 1 strand of dark brown. Backstitch around part of Santa's boot with 1 strand of white (see white line on pattern). With 2 strands of blue, make French knots for Santa's eyes. Use 2 strands of black to make French knots for Rudolph's eyes. Use 2 strands of white to stitch snowflakes in long stitches as indicated on chart.

COLOR KEY

Black	310 DMC
Red	321 DMC
White	Blanc Neige DMC
Yellow	742 DMC
Gold	729 DMC
Light Brown	51c Coats
Dark Brown	81b Coats
Pink	948 DMC
Blue	312 DMC
Light Tan	3024 DMC

Stitch count: 33w×46h
Finished size: 2.36×3.29 inches

3 Following manufacturer's instructions, apply iron-on backing to felt. Trim felt to size and shape of cross-stitched area, making top rounded.

4 Cut ribbon into a 7-inch length and a 5-inch length. To make a hanger, fold 7-inch length in half. Place open ends at top center of back of felt. Following manufacturer's instructions, iron felt to back of cross-stitched fabric.

5 Trim Aida cloth to within 3/8 inch of edge of cross-stitching. Fringe Aida cloth by pulling threads from all sides.

6 Make a 3/4-inch bow from 5-inch length of ribbon. Glue to top center of ornament.

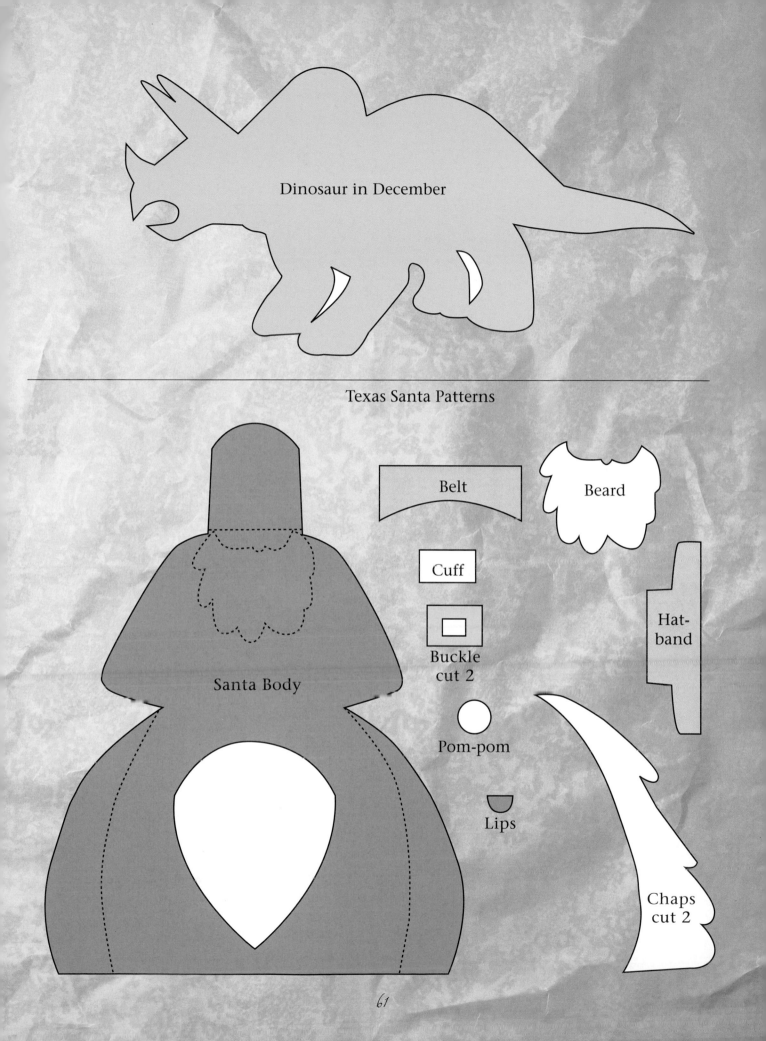

Dinosaur in December

Texas Santa Patterns

Belt

Beard

Cuff

Buckle
cut 2

Hat-
band

Santa Body

Pom-pom

Lips

Chaps
cut 2

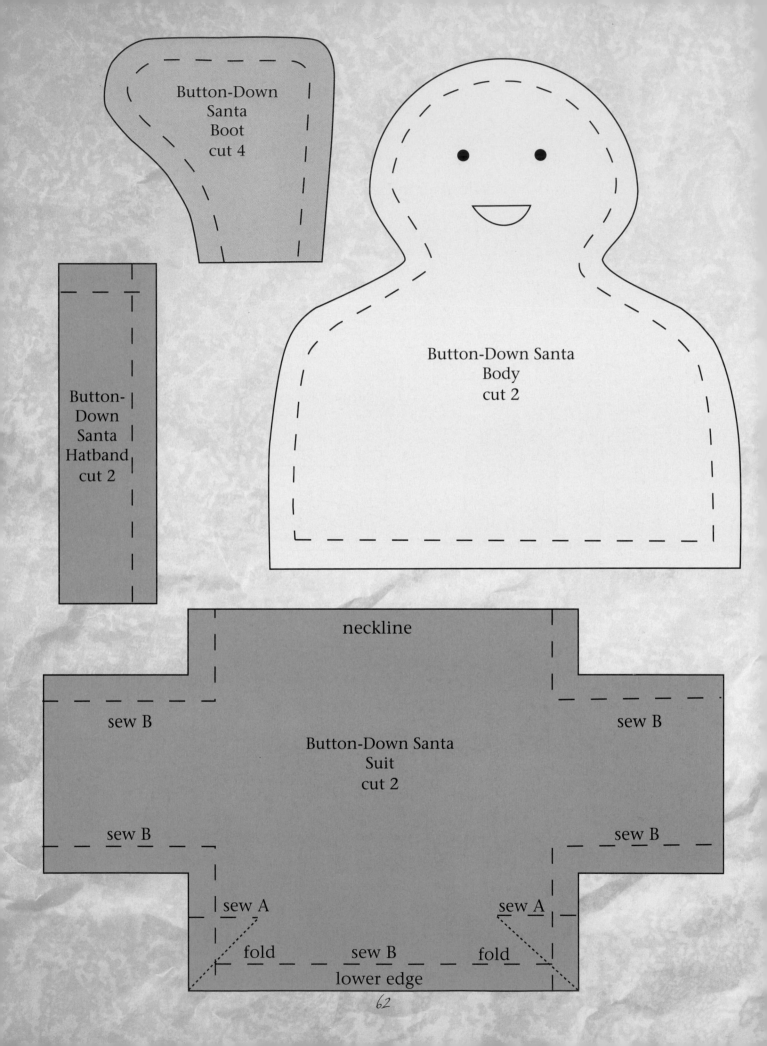

Button-Down
Santa
Boot
cut 4

Button-Down Santa
Body
cut 2

Button-
Down
Santa
Hatband
cut 2

neckline

sew B

sew B

Button-Down Santa
Suit
cut 2

sew B

sew B

sew A

sew A

fold

sew B

fold

lower edge

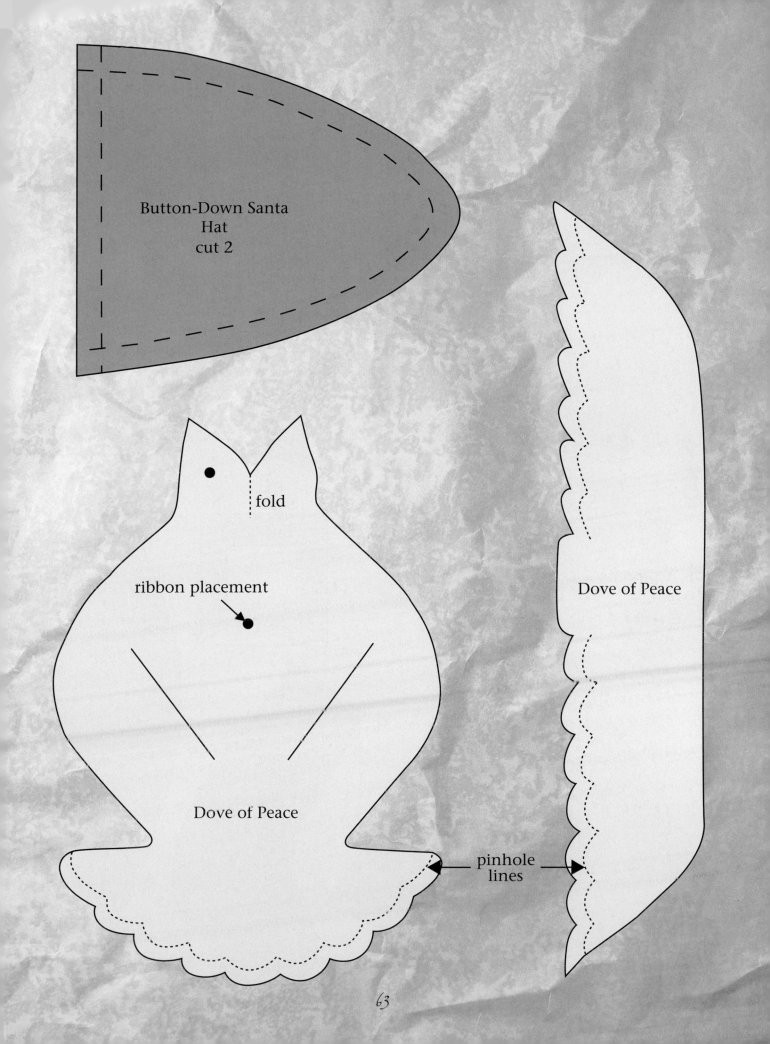

Button-Down Santa
Hat
cut 2

fold

ribbon placement

Dove of Peace

Dove of Peace

pinhole
lines

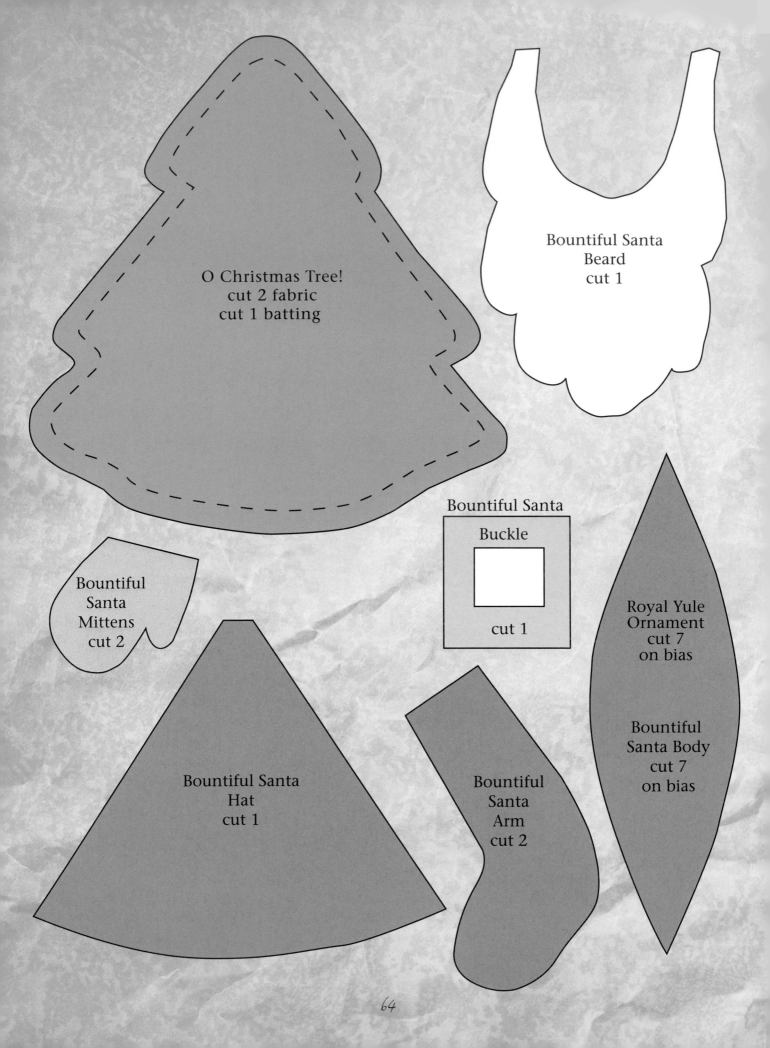

O Christmas Tree!
cut 2 fabric
cut 1 batting

Bountiful Santa
Beard
cut 1

Bountiful Santa

Buckle

cut 1

Bountiful
Santa
Mittens
cut 2

Royal Yule
Ornament
cut 7
on bias

Bountiful
Santa Body
cut 7
on bias

Bountiful Santa
Hat
cut 1

Bountiful
Santa
Arm
cut 2